100 Questions and Answers About Muslim Americans

Michigan State University
School of Journalism

D1402210

Read The Spirit Books

an imprint of
David Crumm Media, LLC
Canton, Michigan

For more information and further discussion, visit
news.jrn.msu.edu/culturalcompetence

Cover art and design by
Rick Nease
www.RickNeaseArt.com

Published by
Read The Spirit Books
an imprint of
David Crumm Media, LLC
42015 Ford Rd., Suite 234
Canton, Michigan, USA

For information about customized editions, bulk purchases or
permissions, contact David Crumm Media, LLC
at info@DavidCrummMedia.com

Contents

Acknowledgments

Students who worked on this guide are: Stacy Cornwell, Amanda Cowherd, Julia Gorman, Lia Kamana, Kate Kerbrat, Sarah King, Kyle Koehler, Arielle Rembert, Zhenqi (Bruce) Tan and Cheyenne Yost.

The project has had valuable help from the following:

Fatina Abdrabboh, director of the American-Arab Anti-Discrimination Committee of Michigan.

Sarah Alfaham, who has a master's degree in social work and is a youth worker and activist in northwest Ohio and southeast Michigan.

Kari Alterman, regional leadership director, American Jewish Committee, and an executive board member of the Interfaith Leadership Council of Metropolitan Detroit.

Wayne Baker, professor of Management & Organizations and professor of sociology at the University of Michigan. He is leading the Americans' Evolving Values project at the Institute for Social Research and is co-author of "Citizenship and Crisis: Arab Detroit after 9/11."

Victor Ghalib Begg, senior adviser to the Michigan Muslim Community Council.

Mucahit Bilici, American Muslim sociologist and the author of "Finding Mecca in America: How Islam Is Becoming an American Religion." He is assistant professor of sociology at John Jay College, City University of New York.

Brian J. Bowe, who holds a Ph.D. in Media and Information Studies from Michigan State University. His dissertation is on media representation of Islam in newspaper stories about mosque-building controversies.

Ustadh Ubaydullah Evans, the first scholar-in-residence at the American Learning Institute for Muslims. Evans has studied at the Institute of Islamic Education and at Al-Azhar University in Cairo.

Allan Gale, associate director of the Detroit Jewish Community Relations Council.

Khalil E. Hachem, cultural diversity trainer and executive editor at Ya Michigan of Bizmagazine.org.

Jaweed Khaleem, national religion reporter at the Huffington Post.

Saeed A. Khan, professor in the Department of History and a lecturer in the Department of Near East & Asian Studies at Wayne State University.

Hussein Rashid, faculty member at Hofstra University and associate editor at Religion Dispatches. He is the convener of islamicate and a contributor to Talk Islam and AltMuslimah.

Dawud Walid, executive director, Council on American-Islamic Relations in Michigan.

Dawood Zwink, executive director, Michigan Muslim Community Council.

Others who helped are John Golaszewski of the Michigan Department of Civil Rights; Thasin Sardar of the Islamic Center of East Lansing; Pembe Yasarlar and Kareemah Abbas at Crescent Academy International in Canton, Michigan; and students at Unis Middle School in Dearborn, Michigan.

About the Series

The Michigan State University School of Journalism designed this series as a journalistic tool to replace bias and stereotypes with accurate information. We create guides that are factual, clear and accessible.

We make these guides by asking people to tell us the questions they hear about themselves in everyday conversations. Some of the questions are simple, but the answers seldom are.

Sometimes, we must interpret the questions to find the meaning behind them. We search for answers in studies, surveys, books and research. We ask experts. Our goal is to answer the first-level questions in ways that are accurate and clear. We respect the people who ask the questions as well as the people the answers describe.

These 100 questions and answers about Muslim Americans do not do justice to a religion that has 1.6 billion followers in more than 100 countries. There is also the complicated confluence of religion, culture, politics and half a dozen other influences. While most Muslims are not Arabs, Arabic is the language of Islam. While we do use some Arabic terms, we generally use the English equivalents.

Our hope is that readers will start with these answers, use the resource section to dig deeper and talk with their Muslim co-workers and neighbors. Each will have different perspectives. True understanding does not come with 100 questions, or even 1,000, but each one helps.

Geri Alumit Zeldes, guide editor, is an associate professor and director of journalism graduate studies at Michigan State University. She is co-author of "Reporting on Islam: A Teacher's Guide." Film credits include "Arabs, Jews & the News" and "The Death of an Imam."

Joe Grimm, series editor, is visiting editor in residence at Michigan State University's School of Journalism.

Foreword

By John L. Esposito

If Muslims were relatively invisible in the West only a few decades ago, today the religious landscapes of most cities and towns include mosques and Islamic centers alongside churches and synagogues. The major Muslim communities and cities of the world today include not only Cairo, Damascus, Islamabad, Kuala Lumpur and Khartoum, but also London, Bradford, Paris, Marseilles, New York, Dearborn, Washington, D.C., Chicago and Los Angeles.

Like many immigrant religious and ethnic minority communities before them, Muslims face challenges in defining and determining their place in society, a secular society whose majority has Judeo-Christian roots. Muslims, like other religious groups, face this question: How do I retain faith and identity and do so in a manner that enables me to also accept and function within the secular, pluralistic traditions of Europe and America?

Muslim minority communities have faced many hurdles in making this transition: issues of faith, identity, citizenship, family and the challenges of living in a pluralistic society. Integral to the experience of Muslims in America, like all religious or ethnic minorities, is the question of integration or assimilation. If the majority of Americans must realize that Muslims are "us," many Muslims struggle with the nature of identity and the relationship of faith to national identity: Are they Muslims in America or American Muslims? The identity of the community and, more specifically, the formation of a new identity in America poses many questions. Can Muslims become part and parcel of a pluralistic American society without sacrificing or losing their identity? Is the American legal system capable of allowing for particular Muslim religious and cultural differences within the Constitution's broader universal claims? Do the secular and/or Judeo-Christian values of American society make it impossible?

The Muslims of America are far from monolithic in their composition and in their attitudes and practices. They are a mosaic of many ethnic, racial and national groups. As a result, significant differences exist in their community as well as in their responses to their encounter with the dominant religious and cultural paradigm of American society.

Regrettably, the legacy of 9/11, continued terrorist attacks, and fears of growing radicalization contribute to a sharp increase in Islamophobia, discrimination against Muslims because of their faith or race, hate speech and violence. Politicians, far-right political commentators, hardline Christian Zionist ministers, and a proliferation of anti-Muslim hate blogs have exploited the situation. They blur the distinction made by presidents George W. Bush and Barack Obama and many other Americans between. On the one hand, there is Islam and the vast majority of Muslims and, on the other, a dangerous fraction of the world's Muslims who, like Jewish, Christian, Hindu, and other religious extremists, hijack religion to legitimize their acts of terror.

Islam is the second-largest of the world's religions and it is the third-largest religion in America. Yet many in the West continue to function within an enormous information vacuum, the same one I myself suffered from more than 30 years ago. When I first encountered Islam in graduate school, I was astonished to discover that there was another Abrahamic faith. We had always talked about the Judeo-Christian connection, but never the Judeo-Christian-Islamic tradition. Why? If Muslims recognize and revere many of the major patriarchs and prophets of Judaism and Christianity (including Abraham, Moses and Jesus) and God's revealed books, the Torah and the Message (Gospels) of Jesus, why had I not been aware of this after all my years of liberal arts and theological training?

"100 Questions and Answers About Muslim Americans" is an important book because it provides an easy-to-read and accurate response to many of the fundamental questions that non-Muslim Americans raise or are concerned about. It enables many who have not had any significant contact with Muslim Americans to begin to understand the faith, practices and values of fellow Americans.

John L. Esposito is professor of Religion and International Affairs and of Islamic Studies at Georgetown University. He is founding director of the Prince Alwaleed Bin Talal Center for Muslim-Christian Understanding and author of "What Everyone Needs to Know about Islam."

Preface

By Mohammad Hassan Khalil

Muslim Americans have long played an important role in the shaping of America. When slave ships coming from Africa docked on the East Coast, they brought with them numerous Muslims whose faith would be tested in the New World. And while some were able to attain freedom and return to their homeland, most would be consigned to a life on foreign land—a land whose overlords generally looked down upon the open practice of Islam. Within a few decades, most African-American slaves of Muslim descent had become Christian. Even so, a small minority managed to hold on to their Islamic faith, if only in private, and without necessarily passing their religious traditions on to later generations.

Seeking respect and a return to the religion of their predecessors during the turbulent civil rights era, many African Americans joined an activist movement called the Nation of Islam. Following the death of its charismatic leader, Elijah Muhammad, in 1975, many members abandoned some of its controversial doctrines (for example, that Elijah Muhammad was a "messenger of God" and that the "white man is the devil") and became Sunni Muslim.

The earliest prominent convert to Islam was Mohammad Alexander Russell Webb (d. 1916), a Caucasian writer and a U.S. consul to the Philippines. Other notable converts include civil rights leader Malcolm X (El-Hajj Malik El-Shabazz) and boxer Muhammad Ali, both of whom joined the Nation of

Islam and then eventually became Sunni Muslims. Basketball star Kareem Abdul-Jabbar, comedian Dave Chappelle and musician Jermaine Jackson are other well-known converts.

Today, most Muslim Americans are either immigrants or the children of immigrants. In the late 19th century, Muslim immigrants—mostly peddlers seeking a new life—began to arrive in droves. At the turn of the 20th century, immigrants performed the first recorded Muslim American communal prayer in—of all places—Ross, North Dakota, where land was relatively inexpensive. Within a few decades, formerly foreign Muslims had established mosques for worship in, among other cities, Biddeford, Maine; Highland Park, Michigan; Cedar Rapids, Iowa; and Michigan City, Indiana. Among the prominent immigrants who arrived in the United States during the middle of the 20th century was Fazlur Rahman Khan, a Bangladeshi-American architect who designed Chicago's Sears Tower, now called Willis Tower, and the John Hancock Center, both American landmarks.

After President Lyndon Johnson signed into law the Immigration and Nationality Act of 1965, the largest-ever wave of Muslim immigrants began to arrive in the United States—a contingent of immigrants that would become wealthier and more assimilated than their counterparts in Europe. Many of these new Americans thrived in both "blue collar" and "white collar" positions. Before long, mosques and Islamic schools were established throughout the country.

For centuries, Muslim Americans, like other American minorities, have had to confront and contend with numerous detractors and misconceptions. One might assume that the horrific attacks of Sept. 11, 2001, only made things worse for Muslim Americans. The sharp rise in anti-Muslim prejudice and hate crimes seems to support such an assumption. Yet it was also after the Sept. 11 attacks that Muslim Americans were elected to the U.S. Congress for the first time (Keith Ellison of Minnesota and André Carson of Indiana); played a more active role in filmmaking ("Mooz-lum"); produced American

Muslim country music (Kareem Salama); and organized major community events open to all (the Chicago-based community program "Takin' It to the Streets"). As such, one could say that the Muslim-American renaissance began on Sept. 12, 2001—resilience after tragedy.

Mohammad Hassan Khalil is an associate professor of Religious Studies at Michigan State University. He is Director of the Muslim Studies Program and author of "Islam and the Fate of Others: The Salvation Question."

Basics

1 How do I say "Muslim?"

Say "Mu," using the "u" sound from "push." Then say "slim." No "oo" or "z" or hissing sound. Correct pronunciation shows respect. Incorrect pronunciation can change meaning.

Follow this link to hear several examples of Muslims pronouncing Arabic words. (http://bit.ly/1v1ivGz)

2 What is the difference between Islam and Muslim?

Islam is the religion. Muslims are the people who follow Islam. The words mean different things. The word Islamic is used to describe teachings, practices and other facets of the religion.

3 Who is Allah?

Allah is the Arabic word for God. Islam, like Christianity and Judaism, is a monotheistic religion, which means followers believe there is only one God. Islam teaches that God is fair and just, has no shape or gender, cannot be seen, always has and always will exist, and knows all. The Arabic phrase "Allahu akbar" means "God is greater" in English. Translations that change all the words except Allah should be avoided. They are incomplete and make it sound as though Muslims worship a foreign God.

4 Who is Muhammad?

To Muslims, Muhammad is the final prophet or messenger
of God. A messenger is a prophet who delivers God's
message to the people. Muhammad was a man and not a
god. He was born in Mecca in 570, Current Era, and died
in Medina in 632. Tradition says that the Archangel Gabriel
began dictating God's message to Muhammad in 610.
This continued for the rest of Muhammad's life. He began
sharing the message a few years after he started hearing
it. The message is the Quran. Muhammad was born into
a wealthy tribe, but his father died before his birth and his
mother died when he was 6. Before she died, she sent the
young Muhammad into the care of others in the desert.
There, away from the city, he learned discipline, nobility
and what it meant to be free. As a man, his generosity and
fairness made Muhammad a source of advice. He delivered
the Quran by dictating it to others, who wrote it down word
for word.

5 How many Muslims are there around the world?

According to the Pew Research Center's Forum on Religion
& Public Life, there are about 1.6 billion Muslims in the
world. This makes Islam the world's second-largest religion
after Christianity, which has about 2.2 billion. Here is
another way to look at it: about one third of the world's
population is Christian; about one fourth is Muslim.

Where do Muslims live worldwide?

		percentage of world Muslim population
1	Indonesia	13.1%
2	India	11.0%
3	Pakistan	10.5%
4	Bangladesh	8.4%
5	Nigeria	4.8%
6	Egypt	4.8%
7	Iran	4.6%
8	Turkey	4.5%
9	Algeria	2.2%
10	Morocco	2.0%

World Muslim Population, 2010

30,000,000   200,000,000

illustration by Cody T. Harrell
source: Pew Research, 2011

6 Where do the world's Muslims live?

Most, about 60 percent, live in Asia. About 20 percent live in the Middle East and North Africa.

7 Are most Arabs in the world Muslim?

Yes, most Arab countries have majority Muslim populations. Some are as high as 99 percent. However, most Muslims in the world and in the United States are not Arabs.

8 How many Muslims are there in the United States?

The Census Bureau does not count religions, so reports vary. The U.S. Council on Foreign Relations reports that estimates range from 2 million to 7 million. The higher estimate would equal about 2 percent of the U.S. population.

9 Are most Muslims in the United States immigrants or native-born?

According to a Pew Research Center study, 63 percent of American Muslims are first-generation immigrants, meaning they came from other countries. Fifteen percent were born in the United States to parents who immigrated, and 22 percent have parents who were born in the United States.

10 What are the major countries of origin for American Muslims?

First- and second-generation immigrants come from about 80 countries. The most common country of origin is Pakistan. Other places include the rest of South Asia, North Africa, Europe and the Middle East, according to Pew research.

Beliefs

11 What are the fundamental components of Islam?

Islam has five pillars, or core practices. These pillars are:

- The declaration of faith: "There is no deity but God, and Muhammad is a messenger of God."
- Prayer. Muslims are required to offer five a day.
- Charitable giving. Muslims who are able will set aside 2.5 percent of net worth to help people in need. Some pay up to 20 percent of their extra income.
- During the month of Ramadan, Muslims abstain from eating, drinking, chewing gum, smoking and intimate relations from dawn until nightfall. Those who are ill and are unable to fast for health reasons or age are exempt, as are women who are pregnant, menstruating or nursing.
- The pilgrimage, called the hajj, which Muslims are obligated to make to Mecca if they are physically and financially able.

12 What is the Quran?

The Quran is the holy book of Islam. Muslims believe it to be the word of God. The book, in Arabic, is a complete record of the words of God revealed to Muhammad through the Archangel Gabriel, who specified how the passages should go together. The Quran is the source of Muslim faith and practice, covering such subjects as wisdom, doctrine, worship and law.

The Five Pillars of Islam

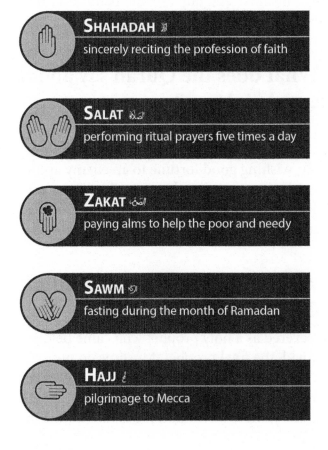

SHAHADAH
sincerely reciting the profession of faith

SALAT
performing ritual prayers five times a day

ZAKAT
paying alms to help the poor and needy

SAWM
fasting during the month of Ramadan

HAJJ
pilgrimage to Mecca

illustration by Cody T. Harrell

13 What is the hadith, and how is it different from the Quran?

The hadith is the record of the words and deeds of Muhammad. The Quran is the word of God. While not held to the same level of importance as the Quran, the hadith is still important because Muhammad is regarded as a model for living God's will. The hadith was passed down through oral tradition and then written down and agreed upon by scholars. Muslims generally use the hadith tradition to discern Muhammad's "way" or example.

14 What does the Quran say about peace and violence?

Various passages in the Quran are interpreted as being both peaceful and violent. There are verses about loving an enemy, wishing good fortune to an enemy and making friends with an enemy, but there are also verses about forcefully defending one's community. Interpreting verses out of context or without research can be problematic.

15 What does the Quran say about Jesus?

Jesus is revered as a holy prophet who came before Muhammad, the final prophet. Muslims do not regard Jesus as God. Stories about Jesus in the Quran are similar to stories in the New Testament, and the Quran mentions his mother, Mary, more often than she is mentioned in the New Testament.

16 Who are Islam's other major prophets?

They include Adam, Abraham, Noah, Joseph and John the Baptist, also recognized by Jews and Christians. Muslims regard Moses, Jesus and Muhammad as messengers who brought God's word to humans.

17 How does one become Muslim?

A person becomes Muslim through the simple declaration or testimony of faith, as stated in the first pillar of Islam. It is a contract between the individual and God. No witnesses or ceremony are necessary, though this can be a way of becoming known as a convert and being welcomed into the community.

18 What is the difference between Shia and Sunni Muslims?

Religious beliefs and practices of these two major branches of Islam are nearly identical. The branches emerged shortly after the death of Muhammad. The split was due to conflicting ideas about succession. Those who said that Muhammad's son-in-law and cousin should be his successor became the Shia branch. The Sunnis believed that any capable Muslim selected by election could lead.

19 Which countries are predominantly Sunni and Shia?

The Pew Research Center estimates the world Sunni population at 87-90 percent of Muslims and the Shia population at 10-13 percent. Most Arab nations have Sunni majorities. Between 68 percent and 80 percent of Shia Muslims live in Iran, Pakistan, India and Iraq.

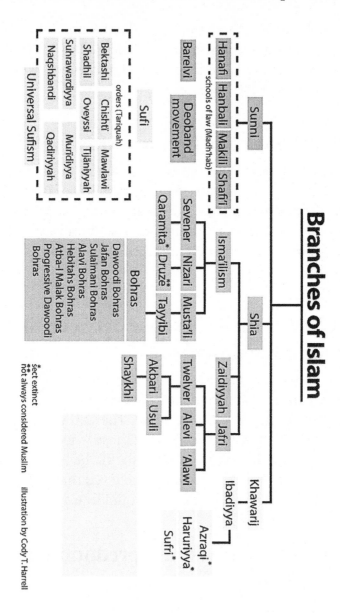

20 Do Muslims believe in an afterlife?

The afterlife plays a large part in the Islamic faith. Islam teaches that on judgment day, humans will be divided between paradise and hell, based on their faith and deeds. The Quran says the best among people are the most pious.

21 Do Muslims believe that non-Muslims are going to hell?

There are differing opinions on this. Some Muslims believe that anyone who believes in God will be received into paradise, while others believe that only righteous Muslims will go to heaven. Some believe that people of Abrahamic religions, also known as People of the Book, will enter paradise if they obey God's will. The divinely inspired books are the Torah, the Gospels and the Quran. Some say those who are unaware of Islam will not be punished for not joining. Islam states that only God decides who goes to heaven and who goes to hell. People are asked to live righteously and to leave God's business to God.

22 What are Abrahamic religions?

Judaism, Christianity and Islam are connected through Abraham. All three faiths consider Abraham a prophet of their God and trace their roots to him and his message of monotheism. All three religions have the same geographical roots in the Middle East and hold Jerusalem as a special place for their faiths.

23 Is the Nation of Islam the same as Islam?

No. The Nation of Islam and Islam have similarities, but they are not the same. Islam teaches that there is only one God, while the Nation of Islam holds that its founder, Wallace Fard Muhammad (W.D. Fard), was the incarnation of God.

24 Does the Quran promote forced conversions?

The Quran prohibits it. Politics and governments have sometimes required conversion to Islam, but this is not the norm globally and does not happen in the United States.

Prayer

25 When do Muslims pray?

Practicing Muslims offer five, prescribed formal prayers a day. Sunnis pray five times a day at dawn, midday, late afternoon, sunset and sometime before midnight. Shias pray three times, combining midday and late afternoon and sunset and evening prayers. Times change as daylight hours get shorter or longer. Schedules and cell phone apps can help people know when to pray. Muslims also pray at other times. They are encouraged to make additional optional prayers.

26 Do the prayers change?

The prayers are consistent from day to day, but it is encouraged they be shortened during travel.

27 Where and how do Muslims pray?

Muslims can pray anywhere that is clean and dry. Some carry a prayer rug to place on the ground. Islam, like many religions, also has ritual cleaning or ablution before prayer. Muslims face Mecca to pray.

28 Why do Muslims pray facing Mecca?

Muslims face Mecca because they were instructed by Muhammad to pray in the direction of the kaaba that Abraham and his son built there.

29 What is the kaaba?

The kaaba is a black, cube-shaped building, about 40 feet tall, in Mecca. Islam's most important mosque was built around the kaaba. Muslims believe that Abraham built the kaaba hundreds of years before the time of Muhammad, whose family belonged to the tribe that cared for the building. The stone kaaba has been rebuilt several times. The "black stone," a relic installed in the kaaba's eastern corner, is believed by some Muslims to be from heaven and to date back to the time of Adam and Eve. The kaaba symbolizes the truth, and Muslims set their compass to the truth no matter where they are. This is why they face the kaaba to pray. There are normally people praying around the kaaba at all times. Pilgrims on hajj pray while circling it seven times.

30 What is the meaning of the initials "P.B.U.H.?"

These letters stand for "Peace be upon him." Some Muslims use these letters in writing or say that phrase after the name of Muhammad, Jesus and other prophets as a sign of respect. In Arabic, the letters might be S.A.W., S.A.A.W. or S.A.A.S.

31 What is the call to prayer and what is being said?

The call to prayer, or adhan, is recited in Arabic by a person called a mu'adin or a muezzin. In Muslim neighborhoods, it might be broadcast over speakers. This is a general translation of the call, though there are differences among countries and branches of Islam:

God is great. (Four times)
I bear witness that there is no god except the One God. (Twice)
I bear witness that Muhammad is the messenger of God. (Twice)
Hurry to the prayer. (Twice)
Hurry to success. (Twice)
God is great. (Twice)
There is no god except the One God.

Practices

32 Does culture influence religious practice?

Yes, and so do politics. People of the same religion practice in different ways and some of their actions have nothing at all to do with religion. The culture of the dominant society where they live can affect how Muslim Americans dress and behave as well as their family values and roles.

33 Why is Arabic dominant among Muslims?

The Quran and the hadith were written in Arabic. Muslims believe the writings are best studied and understood in their original language. This has made Arabic widespread throughout the world, even in countries where Arabic is not a dominant language.

34 Who is the leader of Islam?

Islam has no central authority structure. Titles for leaders vary by country and sect. In the United States, which has Muslims from all over the world, imam and sheik are common. Less common are grand mufti, ayatollah and mullah.

35 Do people have a choice about being Muslim?

Yes, they do. Islam does not force people to join and leaves it up to the individual. Some governments and movements have required membership, and governments in a few countries have made it a crime to leave Islam.

36 What does Islam say about images of God?

Muslims believe it is impossible to know what God looks like, so such images have been discouraged for centuries. This prohibition extends to images of the prophets. Mosques typically do not contain portraits, but often display calligraphy of religious text and geometric designs.

37 What happens in a mosque?

Daily prayers, recitation of the Quran and prayers on Friday, the day mandated for community prayer, all occur there. In the United States, a mosque, masjid in Arabic, can also be a social place, a school and a community center.

38 What should non-Muslims know about visiting a mosque?

Most mosques welcome guests. Visitors should wear modest clothing and remove their shoes before entering the prayer area. In many U.S. mosques, men and women pray in different areas.

39 Why are shoes not allowed in prayer areas?

The prayer area is sacred ground and nothing impure or unclean should be let inside, so shoes are left outside. Muslims perform ablutions, or washing, before entering. This is not usually expected of guests.

40 What is a fatwa?

A fatwa is a legal pronouncement issued by a religious expert. There is no central authority for fatwas. The expert must have rigorously studied the Quran and can issue a fatwa only when aware of all elements of the case. It pertains only to Muslims and is not binding in secular settings. While a fatwa against author Salman Rushdie became one of the most well-known, fatwas calling for the death of an individual are rare. Fatwas usually give religious guidance.

41 What is Shariah?

Shariah is the way or path that Muslims follow to achieve God's will on Earth. It requires Muslims to live righteously, to protect and expand their community and to establish a just society. Shariah describes the ideal relationship between people and God and in their interactions with each other. Shariah's principles come from the Quran, the hadith and other considerations, depending on the sect.

42 What are the major principles of Shariah?

There are six areas of responsibility:

- Respect for life
- Respect for community
- Respect for free enterprise
- Right to political freedom
- Duty to respect human dignity
- Freedom to pursue the path of spiritual knowledge

43 What is Shariah law?

Shariah is Islamic law. Shariah law is the application of these principles to society. It is sometimes confused with Islamic law, which varies according to the circumstances, politics and context of the country where it is implemented. Shariah law is sometimes blamed for brutal punishments such as stonings. These are not the norm.

44 What does halal mean?

Halal means lawful foods, objects and activities sanctioned by Islamic teaching. Halal also refers to foods that are permissible for Muslims to eat and drink. The halal process for slaughter requires that a Muslim invoke God's name and cut the throat with a sharp knife so as to drain the blood. Pork is not sanctioned, no matter how it is processed. Blood, intoxicants and alcohol are not halal, either. Forbidden objects and activities are called haram.

45 Are halal and kosher foods the same?

No. There are similarities, but they are not the same. Because of the similarities, in places where there is a lack of halal food, some Muslims will eat kosher foods, but the foods are not substitutes for each other.

46 Are honor killings a part of Islamic teaching?

No. Islam forbids the killing of any person without lawful reasons. Honor killings are a cultural practice pre-dating Islam in some areas where the religion is practiced, but they are not part of the religion.

47 Is it true that Muslims are not allowed to eat with their left hand?

The hadith tradition encourages eating with the right hand. Not everyone accepts those hadiths. Cultural traditions in many parts of the world have also stressed this practice, though that is changing.

48 What is "the hand of Fatima?"

The hand of Fatima, also known as hamsa, is a hand-shaped amulet popular throughout the Middle East and North Africa. It symbolizes protection. Fatima Zahra was the daughter of Muhammad. It is not a religious symbol and is worn by people of several faiths.

Demographics

49 How long have Muslims been in what is now the United States?

Although it is tough to pinpoint when the first Muslims arrived, their history in North America dates back more than 400 years. Many Muslims were brought to the United States in the slave trade. Today, three quarters of Muslims in the United States are native or naturalized citizens.

50 Where are they concentrated?

According to the U.S. Embassy, Muslims live in every part of the country but are concentrated in major coastal cities and the Midwest. Hubs are New York, Los Angeles, Chicago, and Detroit/Dearborn. The 10 states with the largest Muslim populations are California, New York, Illinois, New Jersey, Indiana, Michigan, Virginia, Texas, Ohio and Maryland. Michigan has the most densely concentrated community of Muslim Americans.

51 How many U.S. Muslims are converts?

According to the Pew Forum's 2007 Religious Landscape Survey, 20 percent of American Muslims are converts to Islam. Sixty-three percent of African American Muslims are converts. Two-thirds of Muslims whose parents were born in the United States are converts to Islam.

Where do American Muslims Live?

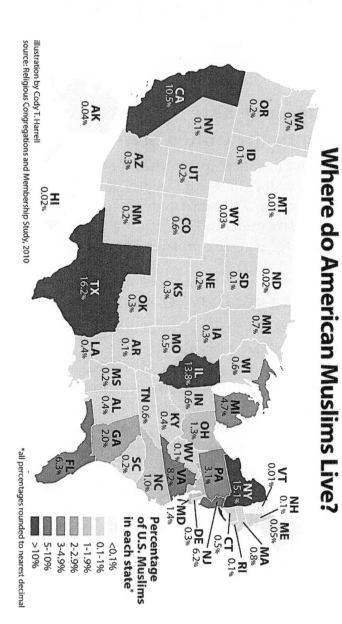

illustration by Cody T. Harrell
source: Religious Congregations and Membership Study, 2010

Percentage
of U.S. Muslims
in each state*

<0.1%
0.1-1%
1-1.9%
2-2.9%
3-4.9%
5-10%
>10%

*all percentages rounded to nearest decimal

WA 0.7%
OR 0.2%
CA 10.5%
AK 0.04%
NV 0.1%
ID 0.1%
AZ 0.3%
UT 0.2%
MT 0.01%
WY 0.03%
NM 0.2%
CO 0.6%
HI 0.02%
TX 16.2%
OK 0.3%
KS 0.3%
NE 0.2%
SD 0.1%
ND 0.02%
MN 0.7%
IA 0.3%
MO 0.5%
AR 0.1%
LA 0.4%
MS 0.2%
AL 0.4%
GA 2.0%
FL 6.3%
TN 0.6%
KY 0.4%
IL 13.8%
WI 0.6%
IN 0.6%
MI 4.7%
OH 1.3%
WV 0.1%
SC 1.0%
NC 1.0%
VA 8.2%
MD 1.4%
PA 3.1%
NY 15.1%
DE 0.3%
NJ 6.2%
VT 0.01%
NH 0.1%
ME 0.05%
MA 0.8%
RI 0.1%
CT 0.5%

52 How many mosques are in the United States?

There are more than 2,100 mosques in the United States. Almost half of American Muslims attend mosque weekly or more. Pew Research suggests that 35 percent of U.S. Muslims are involved in mosque activities outside of religious service. The largest mosque in North America is the Islamic Center of America in Dearborn, Michigan.

53 Is Islam growing in the United States?

Yes. Islam is one of the fastest growing religions in the United States because of immigration, birth rates and conversions. Globally, Islam is growing about twice as fast as other religions.

54 Can you be Muslim and be of another ethnicity or nationality?

Islam is neither an ethnicity nor a nationality. Every Muslim also has ethnic, nationality, cultural and political dimensions, just like people of all faiths. American Muslims are very diverse in this regard. There is no single racial or ethnic group making up more than 30 percent of the total U.S. Muslim population.

What race or ethnicity are American Muslims?

A common misconception is that Muslims are a member of the Arab race. However, the term Arab defines a culture and does not share a direct connection to any specific race. The chart below illustrates the self-identification of Muslim Americans compared to the numbers reflected in the 2010 U.S. Census.

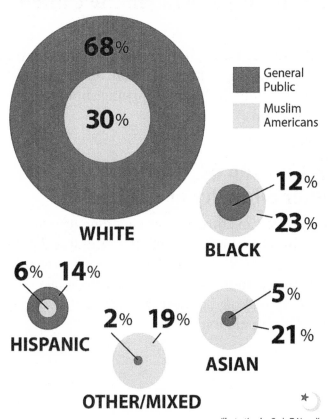

68%

30%

General Public

Muslim Americans

WHITE

12%
23%
BLACK

6% **14**%
HISPANIC

2% **19**%
OTHER/MIXED

5%
21%
ASIAN

illustration by Cody T. Harrell
source: Pew Research, 2011

U.S. Politics

55 How do Muslim Americans align politically?

Currently, most Muslim Americans lean toward the Democratic Party. In 1992, most Muslim Americans voted Republican. A 2008 election exit poll by the Council on American-Islamic Relations found that 89 percent of Muslims favored Barack Obama, while only 2 said they voted for John McCain. In 2012, CAIR reported, more than 85 percent of Muslim Americans voted for Obama.

56 Have Muslims been elected to public office?

Yes. Muslim Americans have been elected to offices from the local level to the U.S. Congress. In most cases, their constituents have been non-Muslim.

57 Who have been some prominent Muslim politicians and political appointees?

- U.S. Rep. Keith Ellison, from Minnesota, became the first Muslim to serve in Congress in 2007. He is a member of the Democratic-Farmer-Labor Party.
- U.S. Rep. André Carson, D-Indiana, elected in 2008.

- Robert D. Crane, former foreign policy adviser to Nixon. Crane was also the deputy director for planning of the U.S. National Security Council.
- Elias Zerhouni, director of the National Institutes of Health.
- Clearance Jack Ellis, former mayor of Macon, Georgia.

Security

58 What does jihad mean?

A jihad means a struggle or effort. Islam has greater and lesser jihads. The greater jihad is to improve oneself through discipline, to live a righteous life and to submit to God's will. A lesser jihad, still important, is to defend one's community and Islam. Some people use the word informally, calling any difficult personal struggle a jihad.

59 Is a jihad a holy war on one's enemies?

That is often a distortion of what it means to defend one's community. Attacks against innocents or seizing others' property are in conflict with righteous living.

60 What does Islamist mean?

This can be a loaded term. The Council on American-Islamic Relations has said that the term is used "in an almost exclusively pejorative context" and has asked that it be used carefully. The Associated Press has said an Islamist is "an advocate or supporter of a political movement that favors reordering government and society in accordance with laws prescribed by Islam. Do not use as a synonym for Islamic fighters, militants, extremists or radicals, who may or may not be Islamists. Where possible, be specific and use the name of militant affiliations …"

61 Do Muslims support terrorist groups?

Most do not. Muslims and Islamic organizations worldwide condemned the 2014 actions by ISIS. Ten years before that, the Fiqh Council of North America issued a fatwa that said, "Islam strictly condemns religious extremism and the use of violence against innocent lives." The Quran itself prohibits religious extremism and implores followers to live moderately.

62 How do Muslims worldwide feel about the United States?

In terms of politics and foreign policy, many people in Muslim-dominant nations don't have very positive feelings about the U.S. government due to actions in the Middle East. They might still be fans of Hollywood or U.S. commodities and culture. This is not a phenomenon occurring solely among Muslims, however. The U.S. image has been sinking around the world. A Pew poll conducted in 2013 found that about 63 percent of people globally felt favorably toward the United States and 33 percent felt unfavorably.

63 How does the conflict over Palestine relate to Muslims around the world?

This is complicated. It is rooted in the history of Palestine and Israel, decisions about the lands made after World Wars I and II and subsequent conflicts. Palestine itself is important to Muslims because of the number of holy sites there. Jerusalem is regarded as a holy city for Muslims after Mecca and Medina, and is regarded by Palestinians as the capital of Palestine.

64 What is the Muslim view of other religions?

The Quran describes Christians, Jews and Muslims, as People of the Book, to be protected and tolerated. Muslims regard Judaism and Christianity as fellow Abrahamic religions.

65 What is Islamophobia?

Islamophobia is fear and prejudice against Muslims based on the idea that Islam is inferior and barbaric and cannot adapt to new realities. It also encompasses the belief that Western and Eastern civilizations have irreconcilable differences in political, economic and social beliefs. Islamophobia existed before Sept. 11, 2001, although attacks on Muslims have grown since then. A 2010 Gallup report found that 48 percent of Muslim Americans said they had been discriminated against in the previous year, and that anti-Islam sentiments had been increasing.

Gender

66 Can women have roles of power?

Yes. To date, several countries have had Muslim women as head of state. They include Turkey, Pakistan, Bangladesh, Indonesia, Senegal, Kosovo and Kyrgyzstan. A Muslim woman's ability to hold power may depend on her country, culture and family. Muslim women also hold important, although perhaps not obvious, positions of power in communities and families.

67 Are Muslim women free to make their own choices?

Again, the scope of a woman's decision-making power depends on country, culture and family. However, most Muslim women make decisions for themselves as well as many important family choices. This is certainly the case among Muslim women in the United States.

68 Why are males and females separated at the mosque?

There are a few reasons for this. The first is that when Muslims prayed behind Muhammad, they would line up the men behind the prophet, then the children, then the women. Modern-day separation emulates this. It gives women privacy and respect when they pray, since Islamic prayer requires bowing and prostrating. Women can feel uncomfortable doing this in front of men. The sexes are also separated to keep worshippers' minds on God and not on human desires.

69 Why do some Muslims decline to shake hands with people of the other sex?

Some Muslims do not touch members of the opposite sex except for relatives, including siblings, parents, children, grandparents, aunts and uncles. Instead, a common form of greeting among Muslims when being introduced is to put the right hand over the heart. Some Muslims make exceptions to non-Muslims to avoid awkward situations. Muslims can touch unrelated members of the opposite sex to help in emergencies.

70 What is the garment that some Muslim women wear on their heads?

The headscarf worn by a Muslim woman is called a hijab. The same word refers to the modest dress code expected of women at the age of puberty and older. Hijab allows women to observe modesty and protect themselves from being cast as sexual objects. It is worn by choice in most places and is more popular in some countries than in others. Culture, politics and government can enter into the issue. The hijab is required in most public places in Saudi Arabia. Iran had banned the hijab in 1936, but made it compulsory in 1979.

How often do Muslim women wear the hijab?

	ALWAYS	SOMETIMES	NEVER
UNITED STATES	36 %	24 %	40 %
EGYPT	62 %	27 %	12 %
INDONESIA	11 %	71 %	18 %
PAKISTAN	32 %	39 %	29 %
TURKEY	56 %	13 %	28 %
NIGERIA	53 %	28 %	15 %

illustration by Cody T. Harrell
source: Pew Research, 2011

71 Do different styles of hijab indicate nationality?

Dress is a mixture of culture and personal preference. Often there is a similarity in the style of hijab between women of the same culture or nationality, but women in the United States choose what they deem modest and in alignment with personal tastes.

72 Do women who wear the hijab play sports or swim?

Yes. Muslim women who cover themselves have competed in high school, college, Olympic and professional sports. There is sportswear and swimwear for women who wear hijab.

73 Are there traditional garments for men?

Modesty is for men, too. While few U.S. Muslim men wear traditional garments, they might choose to stay covered from chest or navel to the knees and to not wear tight clothing.

74 Does Islam condone female genital mutilation?

No. This is not an Islamic practice, but a social custom. The Quran forbids mutilation. A 2013 UNICEF report said that this social practice "is concentrated in a swath of countries from the Atlantic Coast to the Horn of Africa." Some of these are Muslim countries and some are not. Sexual mutilation is uncommon in the largest Muslim countries and some Muslim leaders have condemned it.

75 Does Islam have a position on gay and transgender people?

The majority of Islamic scholars say that the union of two people should be between a man and a woman. However, similar to many Christians and Jews, there are Muslims today who believe that gay and transgendered people can be practicing Muslims and allow them to pray in their places of worship.

Marriage

76 Can Muslims date before marriage?

Many American Muslims do date, but pre-marital relationships were historically not allowed. The process of getting to know one another before marriage can vary according to culture, but the main concept within Islam is there should be a third party present or aware of when a couple is in a relationship to discourage pre-marital intimacy. A comparable example is the courtship process of the early 1900s in America or Britain.

77 Is it customary for Muslim men and women to live at home until they marry?

Some Muslim men and women live with their parents until marriage, but it depends on their country of origin, how long they have been in the United States and whether they have a job.

78 What happens if Muslims have sex before marriage?

In the United States, usually nothing will happen, even though sex outside marriage is technically forbidden in Islam.

79 Do Muslims have arranged marriages?

Some do, but this is not a religious issue. It is more dependent on family upbringing, place of origin and the degree of assimilation. There may be marriages arranged between people who have never met, marriages in which couples are introduced and marriages in which people find each other and seek the parents' blessings. Marriage and having a family are important Islamic values, so parental interest is strong.

80 Can Shia and Sunni Muslims marry each other?

They can and they do. Remember, both are Muslims. Such a marriage would be a closer match than marrying a non-Muslim. Those marriages happen, too, although conservative followers believe Muslim women should not marry outside the religion.

81 Can Muslim men have more than one wife?

The Quran encourages monogamy. In the United States and many other countries, it is against the law to be married to more than one person. Where it is legal, the practice is not widespread. The Quran says Muslim men are allowed to marry as many as four women but only if they can provide for all and treat them equally. The Quran also states that men will never treat multiple wives fairly.

82 May a Muslim marry relatives?

The Quran lists relatives whom a Muslim man cannot marry such as mothers, daughters, sisters, in-laws, stepdaughters, and more.

83 Are genders separated at weddings?

This varies. Wedding ceremonies and receptions are a mix of religion, culture and tradition. Nationality can play a part and, of course, family differences must be accommodated. So, there is no single way or right answer that covers all Muslim weddings. Remember, too, that American Muslim men and women work, shop and travel with members of the other sex all the time. The main time for separation is at prayers.

84 Is music and mixed-gender dancing allowed at Muslim weddings?

This is debated. Even most gender-segregated weddings have music, although it might be only percussion. Such weddings often permit dancing, too. Suggestive music and dancing are discouraged.

85 Can Muslims divorce?

Yes. The percentage of Muslim Americans who report being divorced or separated, 6 percent, is less than half that for the general public, at 13 percent. Marriage rates are almost the same for U.S. Muslims (55 percent) and the public as a whole (54 percent).

86 Can divorced Muslim women remarry?

Yes. Divorced Muslim women are encouraged to remarry, but after a waiting period of at least three months.

Families

87 How large are Muslim families in the United States?

Muslim families in the United States typically span three or more generations. Sixty-seven percent of adult Muslims live in multi-person households. According to Pew, Muslims in the United States are on average younger and have a higher average birthrate, 2.8 births per woman, than the 2.1 rate for U.S. women overall.

88 Are Muslim women permitted to use birth control?

Yes. According to "What Everyone Needs to Know About Islam," the Quran does not address family planning but the hadith does. Some scholars discourage contraception because it limits family size, but most say it is permissible if husband and wife agree.

89 Must Muslim women obey their father or husband?

This aspect of the relationships is largely cultural and familial. In Islam, a marriage is a contract between both man and woman.

90 What are the roles of husband and wife?

In general, there are many roles of husband and wife in an Islamic marriage. Tradition says that the husband's role is to financially provide for his wife, give her shelter and assist her in their quest of salvation. The couple must also be there for each other sexually. There have been different interpretations of Islam's position on housekeeping responsibilities. Of course, present-day realities are changing traditional roles.

91 Are there specific birth rites?

Yes. Typically, the baby's father whispers a call to prayer into the newborn's right ear. After a week, the baby's head is shaved to show that the child is a servant of God. Boys are typically circumcised around this time, as well. Some Muslims have an optional welcoming ceremony for the young child. In tradition, the father might have a sheep slaughtered and share the meat among friends, family and the needy. Today, some families do the equivalent by making donations. They can do this online.

92 Are there rituals when someone dies?

Burials, like weddings, often blend religion and culture. Islamic law mandates that a body be washed and shrouded in white cloth and buried within 48 hours, if possible. Muslims have non-religious cultural traditions, too. During the funeral, loud crying and wailing are discouraged. According to some Muslims, a woman must not mourn for more than three days unless she is mourning her husband.

Muslims believe the dead will remain in tombs until the judgment day, when they will be raised. So, embalming and autopsies are discouraged and cremation is not allowed.

93 What do Islamic teachings say about tattoos and piercings?

Tattoos are discouraged, especially extreme ones, but some Muslims still get them. Scholars have different opinions about this. Muslims are encouraged to be kind to their bodies and tattooing is considered a form of mutilation. Despite this, Simon Baz, an Arab-American character in the Green Lantern comic series, has a tattoo. Baz's tattoo is the Arabic word for courage.

94 Are there coming-of-age ceremonies?

Muslims note maturity with the onset of puberty, so there is not a set age for this. In some cultures, takleef ceremonies celebrate girls entering the age of maturity and putting on the hijab. This is more culturally specific than religiously universal.

Work & Money

95 What educational levels do Muslims attain in the United States?

Educational levels of Muslim Americans are comparable to the educational levels of the general public. A Pew survey in 2007 found that although fewer Muslim Americans graduated high school, the proportion of Muslim Americans obtaining a college degree or attending graduate school was the same as in the general population.

96 What are income levels for Muslim Americans?

Income levels are also similar to those of the general public. Pew found that 41 percent of Muslim Americans reported annual incomes above $50,000, while 44 percent of Americans reported the same. Recent immigrants are more likely to have a higher income than native-born Muslim Americans. The recession that began in 2008 has hurt Muslims more than Americans in general, according to Pew.

97 What occupations or businesses do they work in?

Eighty-eight percent work in the private sector, according to the Arab American Institute. It reports that 64 percent of working Muslim Americans are in managerial, professional, technical, sales or administrative fields.

98 Can Muslims pursue careers in entertainment?

The simple answer is yes, as long as it does not violate Islamic teachings. Many celebrities are Muslim: Akon, DJ Khaled, Ice Cube and more. Things are opening up for Muslim women as entertainers, too. In 2010, the leader of the International Union for Muslim Scholars issued a fatwa saying it was permissible for women entertainers to sing. This conflicted with earlier rulings. Both sides urged women to sing with modesty and to not promote lustful desires. Two popular Muslim women singers are Yuna, of Malaysia, and Deepika Thathaal, who fled her native-born Norway in the face of extremism.

99 What is the Islamic rule about charging interest?

The Quran forbids usury because, at the time it was written, this was seen as exploiting the poor. The idea of not charging interest, then, is related to the Quranic concepts of helping the poor and charitable giving.

100 How do Muslims handle their finances, then?

In the United States, most Muslims rely on the same banking systems as everyone else. Islamic banking institutions might first buy the object, such as a house or car, and have the buyer pay an additional lump-sum amount. Banks might also collect a "late fee" for deferred payments.

Credit sales work under the assumption that the money is being repaid all in deferred payments. In this way, financing is not based on interest.

Holidays

By Stephanie Fenton

The religion of Islam comes out of Abrahamic tradition. Muslims believe that Muhammad (c. 570-632 Current Era) was the final prophet. Though all prophets are revered in Islam, several minor holidays within the religion reflect events in the life of Muhammad. Two major celebrations are recognized universally: Eid ul-Fitr (the Feast of the Breaking of the Fast, at the end of Ramadan) and Eid al-Adha (Feast of the Sacrifice).

To someone following the Gregorian calendar, Islamic holidays appear to slide around from year to year. This is merely an effect, as the Islamic Hijri calendar is a lunar calendar that consists of 354 days (11 fewer days than the solar Gregorian calendar year). The moon's lunar cycles are such a significant element in the Islamic religion, in fact, that significant dates are determined by the visible sighting of a crescent moon. As technology progresses, many experts and organizations are now noting the accuracy of astrological calculations, which place holidays on a universal date. However, many still prefer the traditional method of crescent sighting with the unassisted eye.

Note: Islamic holidays begin at sunset, on the day prior to the dates listed here. Spellings of months, events and holidays, which are translated from Arabic to English, vary widely.

These are the Islamic months, in order:

1. Muharram
2. Safar
3. Rabi'I
4. Rabi'II
5. Jumada I
6. Jumada II
7. Rajab
8. Sha'aban
9. Ramadan
10. Shawwal
11. Dhu al-Qi'dah
12. Dhu al-Hijjah

According to the current Gregorian calendar, notable Muslim holidays are:

Mawlid an-Nabi
Date: The 12th day (and 17th) of Rabi al-Awwal
A birthday celebration for the Prophet Muhammad brings street processions, poetry readings, food distributions and songs to the many Muslim countries that observe this day. Adherents exchange stories and listen to readings about Muhammad's life, focusing on his righteous ways and ability to forgive his enemies.

Not all Muslims observe Muhammad's birthday with such fervor. After all, Muhammad himself asked his followers not to over-emphasize it. Still, many Muslims do mark his birthday, and scholars have agreed that the event bears great importance in Islamic history. Sunni and Shia Muslims usually mark this festival a few days apart.

Good to know: Mawlid an-Nabi is an official holiday in almost every Muslim country, with the exception of Saudi Arabia.

Lailat al Mi'raj (The Night Journey)
Date: The 27th day of Rajab

A journey described as physical, metaphysical and spiritual (opinions vary), Lailat al Mi'raj recalls Muhammad's travels over the course of a single night. On this unique night, Muhammad traveled from Mecca, in Saudi Arabia, to the "Farthest Mosque" in Jerusalem, and then up to heaven, where he met several other prophets and was purified.

The night of these events is divided into two portions. These portions are known, in Arabic, as Isra and Mi'raj. Isra is the journey from Mecca to the Farthest Mosque, and Mi'raj is the journey to heaven. Literally, Mi'raj means ladder.

Most Muslims today attend services at the mosque, relate the story of the "night journey" to children and recite special nighttime prayers. The Farthest Mosque is believed to be at the current site of Masjid al-Aqsa mosque, in the Old City of Jerusalem.

Lailat al Bara'ah (The Night of Records or The Night of Forgiveness)
Date: The 15th day of Sha'ban

A minor holiday replete with sweets and treats gives way to a night of focused prayer, as Muslims prepare for the Night of Records—or, the night that God writes the destiny of each man and woman for the coming year.

Some devotees attempt to stay awake during the night in prayer and worship, and in some places, Muslim communities are lit up with strings of electric lights, candles and fireworks. During the day, charitable giving is a common activity.

Ramadan
Date: The entire month

Arguably the most widely recognized Islamic observance among non-Muslims, the month of Ramadan brings 30 days of daytime fasting and intense prayer. (In some years and in some regions, Ramadan lasts only 29 days, depending on the crescent moon sighting.) The sincerity with which

Muslims undertake Ramadan is reflected in news headlines across the globe. Muslim athletes in the 2012 Olympic Games and players in the 2014 World Cup had to make decisions regarding key competitions and days without a single drop of water. Ramadan requires that every able Muslim refrain from food, drink, smoking, swearing and sexual relations during daylight hours to focus on God and the Quran. Strict fasting during Ramadan is one of the five pillars of Islam.

Muslims fast from sunrise until sunset each day of Ramadan. It is traditional for Muslims to break the daytime fast with three date fruits—just as Muhammad did. The major nighttime meal is known as the iftar, and it often consists of several courses and many dishes. In predominantly Muslim countries, nighttime streets are lively, filled with bright lanterns and packed restaurants. Daytime school and work hours are shortened during Ramadan, and in some regions— such as the United Arab Emirates—it is forbidden even for non-Muslims to eat in public during the daytime hours of Ramadan.

Laylat al-Qadr (Night of Destiny or Night of Power)
Date: One of the last 10, odd-numbered nights of Ramadan

The holiest night of Ramadan is, according to the Quran, "better than one thousand months," in a concept that stretches our comprehension of time and space. Laylat al-Qadr recognizes the night the Quran was first revealed to Muhammad, and though he never provided a precise date, Islam requires that devotees search for it among the final 10, odd-numbered nights of Ramadan. Though observances vary, it is generally accepted by Sunnis that Laylat al-Qadr falls on the 27th day of Ramadan; Shias celebrate Laylat al-Qadr on the 23rd day of Ramadan, as Muhammad did.

In spite of the generally accepted dates, many Muslims attempt to stay awake in prayer as much as possible during each of the odd-numbered nights during the last 10 of Ramadan. Muslims who are able spend the entire final 10 nights of Ramadan in the mosque, where food is provided and a continuous worship is carried out, a practice called I'tikaf. Most Muslims see Laylat al-Qadr as the culmination of Ramadan. This is the period of the most intense prayer, of the greatest giving, the night with the most powerful potential for worship.

Good to know: The Quran was revealed to Muhammad in a series of revelations over 23 years. The initial transmission, recognized with Laylat al-Qadr, began in 610 Current Era in a cave near Mecca.

Eid ul-Fitr (Lesser Eid)
Date: The 1st day of Shawwaal (the month following Ramadan)

The fasting days of Ramadan come to a close with Eid ul-Fitr, the Feast of the Breaking of the Fast. Not only do Muslims not fast on this holiday, it is forbidden for them to do so.

Given that more than one billion Muslims around the world observe Eid ul-Fitr, spellings, start dates—based still, in several regions, on moon sightings—and the length of the festivities can vary widely.

The new Islamic month of Shawwaal begins at sunset. The following day, preparations begin before sunrise. Many Muslims pray, bathe and wear new clothing, stopping only for a small breakfast, traditionally dates, before heading to a mosque, hall or open area. It is recommended that Eid prayers be offered in congregation, so thousands overflow mosques, filling parks and even gathering in fields.

During Eid ul-Fitr, Muslims visit with family and friends, share communal meals and make donations. Festivities can last several days, and fireworks, carnivals, and gift exchanges add to the revelry.

Good to know: The customary greeting on Eid ul-Fitr is "Eid mubarak!" or "Blessed Eid!"

The hajj
Date: Begins on the 8th day of Dhu al-Hijjah

Millions pour into Mecca for one of the world's largest gatherings as Muslims embark on the five-day journey of hajj. The hajj is a religious duty undertaken by every adult Muslim at least once, provided he or she is physically, mentally and financially able, and many Muslims regard hajj as an unparalleled experience. The ritual of a pilgrimage to Mecca stretches back centuries before the advent of Islam, yet it was Muhammad who cemented the rituals of hajj when he made the journey to re-dedicate the kaaba to God. Today, some pilgrims follow the ancient footsteps—literally—by making the pilgrimage by foot.

Pilgrims begin hajj rituals outside Mecca by declaring their intentions for the hajj and wearing the ihram, two pieces of white cloth for men and a white dress for women. Here, participants enter a state of purity, where they cannot harm anyone or anything, argue or challenge anyone. Next, pilgrims proceed to the Grand Mosque in Mecca, where they circumambulate the kaaba—the most sacred location in Islam—seven times, while reciting prayers. This procedure is called the tawaf.

Throughout hajj, pilgrims walk rapidly between the hills of Safa and Marwa seven times; travel through Mina to the plains of Mount Arafat; sleep in tents; mimic Abraham's throwing stones at the devil by casting pebbles at the pillars at Mina; and drink from the Zamzam well, believed to have sprung up at baby Ishmael's feet when Hagar pleaded to God for a source of water. Finally, the pilgrims return to the Grand Mosque to perform tawaf a final time, before departing. This is the day of confession and asking for forgiveness.

Good to know: Major rituals undertaken during the hajj in Mecca focus on Abraham, his willingness to sacrifice his son to God, and events in his family's life.

Eid al-Adha (Greater Eid)
Date: The 10th day of Dhu al-Hijjah

Preparations for this much-anticipated holiday begin weeks in advance. When the day of Eid al-Adha arrives, Muslims enthusiastically wish one another "Eid mubarak!" or "Eid Saeed!" for the Feast of Sacrifice. Recalling the willingness of Abraham to sacrifice his son, Muslims on hajj must sacrifice a halal animal. For Muslims not on hajj, a sacrifice is still recommended. Traditionally, the meat from the sacrifice is split into three: one-third for the family; one-third for neighbors and friends; and one-third for the poor. Those who cannot sacrifice their own animal may pay a company or source to perform the ritual for them.

It is custom for Muslims to arise on Eid al-Adha, dress in their finest clothing and travel to a mosque for Eid prayers, after which they visit with friends and family. Some families present gifts to children during Eid celebrations. Events usually last one to four days, though in some regions, festivities may continue even longer.

The inspiration for Eid al-Adha is Abraham, who received a command from God to sacrifice his son. Though the devil tried to persuade him otherwise, Abraham steadfastly prepared to fulfill God's command. Yet, when he was standing at the altar with blood on his hands, Abraham looked down to see that God had miraculously placed a ram before him; Abraham had slaughtered a ram, and not his son. God had rewarded Abraham's demonstration of complete obedience.

Good to know: This story is also found in the Jewish Torah and the Christian Old Testament (Genesis 22), although in the Jewish and Christian traditions, God asks Abraham to sacrifice Isaac, his son with Sarah. Per Islamic tradition, Abraham was asked to sacrifice Ishmael, his son with Hagar.

Al-Hijra (Islamic New Year)
Date: 1st day of Muharram
In 622 Current Era, Muhammad and his followers departed Mecca and journeyed to the city now known as Medina to set up the first Muslim community. This journey, known as hijra, came to mark the first year of the Islamic calendar. Each year following this journey has been marked "AH"—After Hijra. Though not elaborately celebrated, some Muslims fast and many make resolutions for the year ahead.

Islamic tradition honors Muhammad's demonstration of total devotion to God when he left his family and tribe for Yathrib, the city that would be renamed Madinat un-Nabi, "the City of the Prophet," now Medina. It is believed that during this hijra, Muhammad was fulfilling the work of God in the larger world.

For Shia Muslims, the New Year is marked with solemnity, as they recall the death of Muhammad's grandson, Husayn ibn Ali. Mourning begins on the first night of Muharram and continues for nine more nights until it culminates on Ashura.

Something doesn't add up: The Islamic year consists of 12 months in 354 days (or 355 days, in leap years). The 11- and 12-day difference between the Islamic calendar and the Gregorian calendar means that calculations differ on the number of years since Muhammad's journey.

Ashura
Date: 10th day of Muharram
Two sects of Islam observe Ashura in two very different ways: Sunni, in the centuries-old tradition of fasting; and Shia, in the lament for the death of Muhammad's grandson.

Stretching back millennia, it's believed that Moses fasted to show gratitude for the Israelites' liberation from Egypt, and to this day, Sunnis carry on that ritual on Ashura. Muhammad fasted on this day, and he asked his followers to do the same.

For Shia Muslims, Ashura is about tragedy. Shias believe that Husayn ibn-Ali should have followed Muhammad as the top Muslim leader, and his death in the Battle of Karbala, in an area now part of Iraq, is regarded as treachery. Extreme grief is displayed through mourning attire, the reading of laments and passion plays. Shias believe that Husayn was one of the 12 infallible imams. Mahatma Gandhi voiced the belief that even non-Muslims can gain understanding from the venerable life of Husayn, when he said, "I learned from Husayn how to be wronged and to be a winner; I learned from Husayn how to attain victory while being oppressed."

A former editor with the Detroit area's Suburban Lifestyles Community Newspapers, Stephanie Fenton covered religion for AnnArbor.com. Since 2007, she has provided the nation's only daily coverage of religious holidays, festivals and milestones for ReadTheSpirit online magazine and publishing company.

Resources

Books

Ali-Karamali, Sumbul. *The Muslim Next Door: The Qur'an, the Media and That Veil Thing*. Ashland: White Cloud Press, 2008. Print.

An-Na'im, Abdullahi Ahmed. *What is an American Muslim? Embracing Faith and Citizenship*. Oxford: Oxford University Press, 2014. Print.

Bazzy, Najah. *The Beauty of Ramadan: A Guide to the Muslim Month of Prayers and Fasting for Muslims and Non-Muslims*. Canton: David Crumm Media, 2008. Print.

Bilici, Mucahit. *Finding Mecca in America: How Islam is Becoming an American Religion*. Chicago: The University of Chicago Press, 2012. Print.

Brown, Jonathan A.C. *Misquoting Muhammad: The Challenge and Choices of Interpreting the Prophet's Legacy*. London: Oneworld Publications, 2014. Print.

Council on American Islamic Relations. *American Muslims: A Journalist's Guide to Understanding Islam and Muslims*. Washington, D.C.: CAIR, 2009. Print.

Esposito, John L. *Islam: The Straight Path*. 4th ed. Oxford: Oxford University Press, 2011. Print.

Esposito. *What Everyone Needs to Know About Islam*. 2nd ed. Oxford: Oxford University Press, 2011. Print.

Esposito and Dalia Mogahed. *Who Speaks for Islam? What a Billion Muslims Really Think*. Washington, D.C.: Gallup Press, 2008. Print.

Khalil, Mohammad Hassan, ed.: *Between Heaven and Hell: Islam, Salvation and the Fate of Others*. Oxford: Oxford University Press, 2013. Print.

Khalil: *Islam and the Fate of Others: The Salvation Question.*
Oxford: Oxford University Press, 2012. Print.

Matlins, Stuart M. and Arthur J. Magida. *How to Be a Perfect Stranger: The Essential Religious Etiquette Handbook.*
Woodstock, Vermont: SkyLight Paths, 2010. Print.

Pintak, Lawrence and Stephen Franklin. *Islam for Journalists: A Primer on Covering Muslim Communities in America.* Pullman: The Edward R. Murrow College of Communication, Washington State University, 2013. Digital.

Qazwini, Hassan, compiled by Joffer Hakim. *Handbook of Every Day Islam: Answers to the Most Commonly Asked Questions Concerning the Faith of Islam and its Followers.*
Dearborn: The Islamic Center of North America, 2013. Print.

Websites

Gallup: http://www.gallup.com/poll/104629/who-muslims.aspx

Islamicity: http://www.islamicity.com/

National Endowment for the Humanities: Muslim Journeys Bookshelf: http://bridgingcultures.neh.gov/muslimjourneys/

Oxford Islamic Studies Online: http://www.oxfordislamicstudies.com/

Pew Research Center: http://www.pewforum.org/2013/04/30/the-worlds-muslims-religion-politics-society-overview/

Pew Research Center: http://www.pewforum.org/2009/10/07/mapping-the-global-muslim-population/

Organizations

Association of Indian Muslims of America: http://www.aimamerica.org/

Council on American-Islamic Relations: http://www.cair.com/

Fiqh Council of North America: http://www.fiqhcouncil.
org/
Islamic Center of America: http://www.icofa.com/
Islamic Society of North America: www.isna.net/

Also in This Series

100 Questions and Answers About Indian Americans
100 Questions and Answers About Americans
100 Questions and Answers About East Asian Cultures
100 Questions and Answers About Hispanics and Latinos
100 Questions and Answers About Arab Americans
100 Questions, 500 Nations: A Guide to Native America

If you enjoyed this book, you may also enjoy

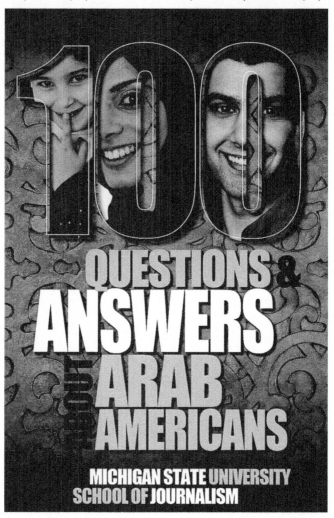

This questions and answers guide from the Michigan State University School of Journalism provides 100 answers to basic questions about Arab Americans.

http://news.jrn.msu.edu/culturalcompetence/

978-1-939880-56-7

If you enjoyed this book, you may also enjoy

This questions and answers guide from the Michigan State University School of Journalism provides 100 answers to basic questions about East Asian cultures.

http://news.jrn.msu.edu/culturalcompetence/

ISBN: 978-939880-50-5

If you enjoyed this book, you may also enjoy

This questions and answers guide from the Michigan State University School of Journalism provides 100 answers to basic questions about Indian Americans.

http://news.jrn.msu.edu/culturalcompetence/

ISBN: 978-1-939880-00-0

If you enjoyed this book, you may also enjoy

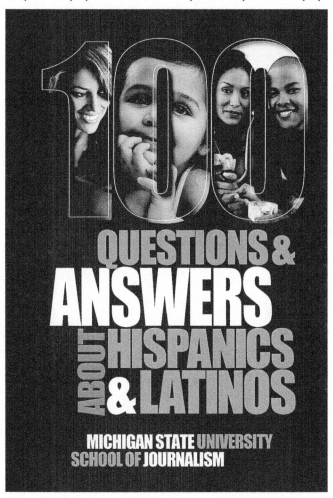

This questions and answers guide from the Michigan
State University School of Journalism provides 100
answers to basic questions about Hispanics and Latinos.

http://news.jrn.msu.edu/culturalcompetence/

ISBN: 978-1-939880-44-4

CPSIA information can be obtained at www.ICGtesting.com
Printed in the USA
BVOW08s2300160116

432930BV00008B/69/P